LIFELONG MARRIAGE IN THE GREATEST GENERATION

Linda G. Bell, Ph.D.

DEDICATION: **To David, my lifelong marriage partner**

PREFACE

The focus of this book is the "greatest generation," couples who grew up during the depression and married after WWII. It is based on a longitudinal study which looked at these couples' lives growing up, marrying, having a family. The book is based on interviews, first at mid-life, then in elder life (some 25 years later). The exercises were typed, then coded for various marital health issues. During the initial home interview, couples completed a discussion of differences in their opinions about the family. They repeated this exercise when they were interviewed in elder life. During the elder life interview, the couples also discussed their relationship history and their ideas as to what was necessary for a successful marriage.

These couples grew up in poverty for the most part. In their time, divorce was considered to represent failure on the part of the partners. Almost all people felt that divorce was not an option. The couples had no self-help books to guide them. They strongly valued commitment, toughing it out, and working it out. It is hoped that learning about them, their values, their lives, their struggles, can be helpful to others who seek to create lifelong marriages. They grew up and lived their lives in a world very different from today's. They speak here from wisdom acquired through long experience and struggle.

Each generation grows up in its own historical context. In many ways these couples' life experiences seem very different from ours today. Their generation was less educated and less wealthy than we are today. There were no cell phones; there were no TVs. Yet, they may have something to teach us about endurance, commitment and success in marriage. The first part of this book looks at these couples' life experiences: growing up in the depression, how they met and married, the struggles and supports they had in their marriage. The second part summarizes their ideas about what makes for a good marriage.

ACKNOWLEDGEMENTS

Primary thanks go to the couples who welcomed us into their homes and completed the interviews. Also to the students and research assistants to helped with the interviewing and the coding. Original funding for the project was from the National Institute of Mental Health. Additional grants were received from the University of Houston – Clear Lake and the Texas State Coordinating Board for Higher Education

To grow mature is to separate more distinctly, to connect more closely.

Hugo von Hofmannsthal, The Book of Friends, 1922

CONTENTS

PART I: THE COUPLES AND THEIR CONTEXT

Life-long commitment is an ideal and a goal for many people going into marriage. Marriage is good for you. As Linda Waite and Maggie Gallagher point out in their book, *The Case for Marriage* [11], married people are happier, healthier, and better off financially. They live longer and have more sex. In our research, couples who had healthier marriages and families at mid-life had kids who were healthier as adults [4]. And they, themselves, were healthier both physically and psychologically in elder life, with more supportive and respectful relationships with their adult children [3]. However, many marriages fall short of ideals and hopes. This book will look in detail at couples who married and stayed married for life. We will explore how they did it.

For the most part, the couples studied for this book were born during the Depression and married after World War II. About a fourth of the wives and husbands had at least one parent who was an immigrant from Europe. These parents came from

Germany, Russia, Denmark, Finland, Sweden, Yugoslavia, Poland, Belgium, Czechoslovakia, Italy, Hungary, Latvia, Lithuania, Austria, England, Holland, Greece and Ireland. Many people in our sample grew up in ethnic neighborhoods or were very aware of people's ethnic backgrounds. About a third of the couples had parents who did not attend high school; half graduated high school; only 10% graduated from college. Educationally, the couples themselves achieved much more than their parents. Ninety-five percent graduated high school; 25% graduated from college. When we first interviewed these couples, in the mid-1970s, they were parents of teenagers. We interviewed them twice 25-30 years later, first by phone, talking with them about their personal well-being, and their relationships with their adult children [1]. This was followed by the home interviews which included a discussion of their lives and their ideas about marriage.

Chapter 1

Growing up during the Great Depression

It is hard, if not impossible, for us to imagine today the depths of poverty common to many Americans during the Great Depression of the 1930s. Economic stress created social stress. Many men left their families to look for work. About two million people were homeless and transient. A million families lost their homes. Many families "doubled up," with two families sharing space previously occupied by one. My own parents were fortunate in that they did not lose their jobs, but like most who continued to work, their pay was cut. They coped by giving up their one bedroom with bath apartment and moving into a boarding house where they shared a bath with another family. Married in 1931, they also decided not to have children – another common decision for couples coping with the times. Both marriage and birthrates declined during the depression. Poverty also contributed to rising ill health, and to increasing malnutrition, disease, and even death because of insufficient medical care [10]. Prior to the depression, health insurance was unknown, likewise any government programs to help the poor. Many people simply could not afford medical care. Social Security, a lasting legacy of these years, was created in 1935 to help the elderly.

Here are some of the stories from these men and women. In the quotes, wives' answers are italicized; husbands' are not. Some details were changed to increase clarity and/or to maintain anonymity. I use bold versus plain text to separate couples.

> I was born and raised on a farm and of course it was depression time, so we had very little outside of what we grew. We did eat well. We had our vegetable garden and we were able to butcher, so we had meat. We had no electricity or refrigeration and that was pretty tough. Yea, it was hard going. At that time it was all horse drawn and you had harness horses and it was quite a chore to hook 'em up. We finally graduated to tractor, but that was after the war [World War II]. In 1939 we moved to a farm that had power, that had electricity, and that made quite a difference for us. And about that time I started high school and eventually was drafted into the service.

I remember an awful lot of anger and a lot of pain because my parents disagreed a lot. We had extended family; with the depression and everything, everybody had to move in together. My parents were only married two years when my grandmother, grandfather and about four aunts moved in, and my father's goal was to have our family get their own place. But my mother felt a certain loyalty to her own parents. She was worried about them and that caused a lot of friction. On other hand, on the positive side, my parents were always there. They were so steadfast in their love; they never showed any love, demonstrative love by hugs or kisses, but we were very aware that they both loved us even though their own relationship had difficulties.

I grew up in a fairly strict household. My dad was a policeman and he saw a lot of kids getting into trouble and things like that. So we were pretty well restrained as children, my brother and me. It was a loving household. We worked hard. My mom worked very hard; she was a beautician. She did it part time; she had a beauty shop in the basement, and she used to be running up and down, doing somebody's hair and making dinner. I mean she was a very, very busy lady, trying to make ends meet. My dad didn't make a very good salary as a policeman. He took the job only because he knew the depression was coming, and policemen were going to be paid. So he took care of our family, his mom and dad and my mom's mom and dad, because he was the only one that was making any money.

While the couples told stories of hardship, they also shared many good memories.

I would say that I had a relatively happy childhood. We stayed in the same neighborhood and we had a lot of friends whom I still have. We were poor. My parents worked very hard to keep things going as a family, but as a child I don't think that I was very conscious of it. Most of

**In my case, my father died when I was
six. So my mother essentially raised me
with some help from my older sister.
Mom raised two kids on her own and
without any education. This was back in
the 1930s so there was no social
security; it was right after the
depression. We did get help like from
the Salvation Army, dental service, teeth
taken care of, clothes. We lost the
house when my dad died. So it was a
little rough for a few years, but we came
though it and, I think, turned out all
right, both my sister and me. I had lots
of friends that I grew up with and overall
it was very good. I'd say I had a very
happy childhood.**

Many people mentioned that they felt safer then; that kids
were freer, parents less fearful.

*I'm very happy that I lived in the time span
that I did. I think of that as the best time. I
felt very secure and safe all the time. And*

basically, I was free to do whatever I wanted. And I don't mean when I was a teenager, because you're not free as a teenager. But as a young child we had friends, you went outside and you played, and you didn't have to worry about anything. And there was nothing to be concerned about – so carefree and happy. You were protected.

We were safe in our community because my family moved around, especially during the war. But wherever we went, you could walk to the store or you could go to the park or wherever.

I spend most of my childhood in the park. I would get up in the morning and all I had on my mind was to go and play in the park all day. It was just a block away. My mother would even pack me a lunch so I wouldn't have to come home. If she wanted me, she would whistle and if I didn't hear it, someone else would, and they'd say, "Your mom is whistling." When you heard the whistle, you knew to come home. Most of the family knew everybody on the street.

> You had to be careful what you did because the neighbors would tell on you. Everyone watched out for everyone else. There was a saying, "When the streetlights came on, then you came home."

Grandparents were very important to many of these people, especially when their grandparents lived with them and both parents worked.

> *I just remember we lived in a house and my grandparents lived upstairs. My grandmother was very influential in my life because she taught me cooking and homemaking kind of things, whereas my mother was working periodically on and off. Either I'd go upstairs, or my grandmother would come downstairs. There was a little landing on the way to the second floor. We had a refrigerator on the landing and shared it. I do remember that.*

It seems like a different world.

> *I was the youngest of two girls. My mother would've liked to have had more children,*

but my dad said no and that we couldn't afford any more. So they had two. My dad graduated from high school and started working at eighteen. He never had formal education, but always took courses when they were offered through work and worked for one company for forty-two years. And he worked his way up. And my mother, I don't think she even had high school. She came from a very poor family; very hard time. My mother was married at seventeen and my dad was twenty. So they were just kids. And my sister was born a year after that and I came four years after that. And I was the first one in the family that ever went to college and they were very proud of that. I didn't end up finishing because I met my husband. Growing up we always went to church on Sundays. We kids went to Sunday school. My mother was the Sunday school superintendent for years. We didn't have a lot of money and didn't get to do things like piano lessons, dancing and things like that. But we kids were always playing baseball, riding our bikes or our scooters. We made things a lot.

Nothing was organized like Little League and all that. We had all our own teams. We lived in a neighborhood full of kids and we were always outside playing.

Some people recounted stories of abuse or neglect; others talked about warm affection from parents; the most common theme was loving parents who did not show much affection, "no hugs and kisses and stuff like that in our house." People's experiences as children contributed to the kind of relationships, they were able to create later in life. Wives who were able to report that their mothers really cared for them had healthier marriages of their own. Husbands who reported that their mothers were dissatisfied with them or that she blamed them for her problems grew up to have less healthier marriages. The good news is that the marriages got healthier as the couples grew older. Compared with the mid-life marriages, the elder couples enjoyed more affection and more respect. There was more warmth and support. Also more comfort with individual differences and less underlying conflict [1],

Chapter 2

Marriage

Most of these couples married young. Many married right out of high school, others during college or after graduation, some after the man came home from military service. They knew each other as children or were introduced by friends. The most common answer to "How did you meet?" was "on a blind date." There were lots of references to dancing and bowling in their courtship stories. A couple of men mentioned that they had to get parental permission to get married because they were under 21 years of age. This was a legal requirement for men. Divorce was less common, and less accepted, than it is today. Again, in the quotes, wives' answers are italicized; husbands' are not.

> I followed her home from school one day; she was the new kid in the class. I found out she lived right next door to me. This was 5th grade. Things evolved in a strange way because she was the valedictorian of

the class and I was the sweat hog. But I got along very well with her younger brothers, and we played together consistently, and she wouldn't give me the time of day. We were on and off in high school, but we went to the junior and senior proms together. Then I went away to college and she went to a school near home. But after 2 years we decided that wasn't working so we got engaged and got married between junior and senior year.

We went to the same high school. Small town. We grew up together; lived next door to each other. He was in the grade with my older sister.

I worked with a man who was his best friend. So he invited my girlfriend and me to come to a bar that they hung out in, and he introduced us. When I first saw her, I shrugged her off. I was too independent. Another day, she dropped in and we started dancing, and we got together after that.

We worked in the same company, different offices. Friends hooked us up on a blind date. We knew each other for 3 months and then got engaged for one week and then married. We had to speed up the wedding because I got drafted for the army. Just immediate family; no friends; very rushed.

We were both in a bowling league. I bowled in the ladies' league which bowled first, then his league bowled after mine and that's how we kept running into each other. We had a small wedding, with family and a few close friends at a Swedish club banquet hall. It was very nice. I had a white dress and he had a blue suit that his sister had to cut open the pockets.

We met at a neighborhood dance hall after I was out of the service. *Neighborhood dance halls were very common in those days. And it was safe; there weren't the risks involved that there are today. He came up and asked me to dance and his Texas accent got me right away. So we went for pizza*

after the dance and he took me home. He gave me a kiss on the forehead. Two months later we were engaged.

We met in college. He was just back from Korea. The Vets were the definite thing then. We dated six months and married; I was 19 and he was 22. We had a small wedding to save money, but my father's family got real mad because we didn't invite all the cousins. Dad had a big family. We just had family and a few close friends, about 100 people.

We met at a bowling alley and started dating. We had a church wedding. She's Catholic and I'm Protestant so in those days they had us on rules, and so I had to agree to raise the children Catholic, which I didn't have a problem with. We had a small reception, dinner for our family and friends.

We lived a block apart and we both attended the same church. We met in the youth group at church; we were both in the choir, too. *I was 16 and he was 17. We dated for three years.* It was funny because when we got married, she could get married, but I had to have my mother sign for me because I was only twenty. I had to have her permission to get married.

Weddings were usually in a church, sometimes at home. Most commonly, there were about 100-150 friends and family at the wedding. A small wedding seems to have been about 100 people or less; 200 or more was considered to be a large wedding. While many in this generation had two or three siblings, their parents usually came from very large families, so they had lots of aunts, uncles and cousins. A reception after the wedding often involved dinner and dancing. Several talked about the heat and humidity; there was no air conditioning.

Church wedding. I was in the military and came home for the weekend to get married. Nice wedding, parents, brothers and sisters, cousins, godmother. All I remember was that there was no air conditioning. The honeymoon waited until later, when I got out of the military.

We were high school sweethearts. When I was a freshman, he happened to be in one of my classes, and he doesn't like to hear this, but I said 'now that's the one' during the first week. Two years later he asked me out. We dated through college—he went to college; I went to work. Very hot day for the wedding and the hall wasn't air conditioned. 150 people. Family and friends. Parents, grandparents, aunts. Humid and hot. It rained in the morning and we were married at four in the afternoon, so it was really steamy by then.

Ethnicity and religion were salient issues for many in this generation. Many identified with the countries from which their parents had immigrated; many lived in communities made up of people from their own ethnic background. Several mentioned that if one were Catholic, the other had to agree to raise the children Catholic.

We met when I was in college and she was on the rebound. *That was my last year of high school. He gave me the ring for my*

18th birthday; I graduated in June and we married in September. Grandparents on both sides were immigrants. Her mother didn't want me to marry her daughter because I was Polish. *Well, in those days you were marrying in your ethnicity and your religion. But I was Slovak, and he was Polish, which are very similar by today's standards! We ended up getting married even though my mom wasn't thrilled about it. My parents never encouraged me to go to college. Your goal in life was supposed to be to get married, have children, and lead a good life. Women didn't have careers, but we did have jobs.*

It was common for both parents to work until the first baby was born. Many wives then stayed home for the kids, at least until the youngest was out of elementary school. But there were also many three-generation households, which allowed Mom to work while Grandmother stayed home with the kids. Many of these couples took care of elderly parents, having parents live with them for many years, even prior to illness.

You might say our marriage was kind of arranged way back then. I'm not gonna say that I fell in love with him cause I didn't. I mean at the time I was only like fifteen and my father was very close with his brother and his family and my father really liked him, I mean <u>really</u> liked him. And my father said, "He's a good man and you'll have a good life and I really think you should consider." And I mean being fifteen at the time was like, way back then anyways, you didn't think of marriage. But it's like he knew what was best for me. And he was right, and things started happening.

I was lucky that I could stay at home with the kids. I stayed home until the youngest was in junior high. But today that's not a choice. I see the young girls at work who can't afford to be a stay-at-home mom.

When I got pregnant, I had to stop working; when they found out you were pregnant, you had to quit. I remember my sister was married during the war and she had to keep it a secret because she worked for the electric company, and they didn't allow married women to work.

My mother lived with us for twenty years. She moved in shortly after my dad died. First, she went to my brother, then came here with us. In a way she was a big help because my wife wanted to go back to work. So with Grandma here, she was here when the kids came home from school. And when we came home, often dinner was on the table for both of us. She had her own privacy downstairs and her own TV. And the kids were close to Grandma, too.

Chapter 3

Some Survived; Some Thrived

Let's put it this way. If we had been married fifteen, twenty years ago, we probably wouldn't be married because of the hard times we had and the big problems we had at the beginning of the marriage. We didn't divorce because it wasn't done that much back then. Now it's nothing. I mean why stick together? Both people are working, both people have incomes. I think that it is very difficult for anyone to have a good marriage now. Very lucky for the ones that do.

During the first home interview, couples did an exercise in which they discussed different opinions about the family with each other. The discussion was recorded. The discussion was then coded; their relationship was described by outside coders on a number of variables which can be summarized as high or low on affection and on respect. Affection is associated with a warm, loving relationship; this kind of relationship usually includes high levels of trust. Respect has to do with acknowledging and validating each other as individuals with their own idea and feelings [2].

Couples high in affection and high in respect. Many of the couples we interviewed scored high on both affection and respect. They seemed to have achieved a good life for themselves and their children. Children grew up in homes where their parents loved each other and parented well. There was warmth and humor. Mates were acknowledged as unique individuals with their own thoughts and feelings. There was no "If you disagree with me, it means you don't love me." Feelings were expressed, including sad and anxious feelings. For most couples, when there were different opinions, it was OK to disagree, recognizing that different people have different experiences. The following quotes are from couples in marriages coded as high on both affection and respect. In the quotes, wives' answers are italicized; husbands' are not.

We both worked, and we've been very fortunate. Our main support was each other, and the children. Also friends, and my sister, and my mom and dad. I think a positive attitude is important, and faith in God to help you through the hard times.

I ***think what you have to do is be respectful of your spouse's attitudes and feelings; And you've gotta be flexible. If you're wrong, say 'I'm wrong." And when you do something, you've got to apologize.***

It's important to trust one another, to communicate, talk over problems and try to solve them, and basically just being able to laugh at yourself.

Of course we argue; everybody does, and everybody disagrees. **You've gotta resolve your problems, your disagreements – don't let them turn into problems. A problem is something you can't really solve. But the difference of opinion, or a minor disagreement, or**

whatever you want to call it, if you can solve it, then it's not a problem.

Our main support was each other. *I think we were open with each other, and he knew that I was behind him one hundred percent; I did the best I could to keep his spirits up when he was getting low because of stuff at work or problems in his family.*

It's important to note that some couples, even though they had very difficult childhoods, were still able to create loving, stable marriages and families. How did they do it?

We didn't have support systems; just each other. We're it.

We wanted to give our children a loving, close family, to listen to them. *We went through some rough times financially, but once things picked up, we were able to give our kids a great education.*

The secret to marriage is hard work and tolerance. You have to work very hard at it; you can't take it lightly. *He worked a lot and we'd talk when he got home so I could tell him what was happening with the kids.* The people I work with would never understand. They were drinkers; a lot of them were drinkers. They would go to the bar after work and they'd sit there. They'd say, "come to the bar and have a drink", I'd say, "no, I'm going home." I always knew I had a hot meal waiting for me. Two o'clock in the morning and it would be sitting on the stove. Always. *That's what I mean by talking.* We'd sit in the kitchen -- *talking.* Sometimes at midnight, two o'clock in the morning. And we'd sit there and talk while I ate my meal and that's when we would find out what's been going on (both laugh).

A lot of people today, if it becomes too difficult or uncomfortable, they get out. And you can't do that. *A lot of what I find is the "me, me, me syndrome." They don't think about the other person. They just think of themselves, and if they're uncomfortable, they want out. They don't try to work it out.* We grew up in a generation where there wasn't any "me." You were lucky if there was anything. My father lived through the Depression and had to start all over again. That stays with you a long time, and it

changes you attitudes. My family struggled to a great extent; in later years my father was ill, and my mother had to go to work late in life to support the family. And there were times that we had a hard time putting food on the table. But we always managed, and we didn't think anything about it.

<u>Couples high in affection and low in respect.</u> In some couples, mates had a high level of affection. They were warmth and caring, but they were did not acknowledge disagreements. They expected one another to hold to common values, beliefs, opinions, and feelings. These mates appeared to genuinely care for each other. But perhaps they were overly close; they denied having any conflict or anger. Here are some of their comments.

> *My mother took interest, but it was tough for her because my dad died when I was quite young, so she was the breadwinner. So she really didn't have the time to get involved in a lot of things. Those things she could come to, she was there. I had a really*

good relationship with my mom. Mom was a special lady.

I remember being lonely as a child; but I had these friends next door, and their mother was a wonderful woman, and she'd take me with them when they went to the movies.

The secret of a good marriage is a need for each other, closeness, being good friends. You can be selfish, just ignore each other. Sometimes I feel like I'm slipping into being selfish, and I just gotta step up.

***Just enjoy being together. I mean comfortable, secure.* Try to pick out things that both of you like to do; find a middle ground.**

The secret to a good marriage is humor; don't be self-centered. *I believe in loving somebody; if you don't love somebody, then I don't see how it could possibly work*

<u>Couples low in affection and high in respect.</u> Some couples were neutral or a little 'cool' in their affect, showing less

affection, less touching, less warm cozy climate. However, there were high levels of mutual respect. Individual ideas and feelings were acknowledged and respected. These couples appeared somewhat cold, somewhat sad, with almost no humor. Oh the other hand, they were good negotiators; good at problem-solving and conflict resolution. Comments by mates in this group often focused on hardship growing up:

> My dad was in the service; then he got sick, so my mother raised me. We were poor, but we were loved. And we were no worse off than anybody else at that time.

> ***My childhood was very rough. My parents divorced; my stepmother beat me. A nurse noticed that I was malnourished, so I ended up in an orphanage. There were some nuns that beat the heck out of me, too.***

> *In marriage, you have to agree on what you want, and you have to do things with your kids.* We both worked hard, worked long hours, but now we have money to help our kids out.

What comes to mind for me is the pain I felt as a child, in being part of my family. I didn't feel wanted and I didn't feel appreciated or valued. I felt like I was a mistake and that everything I did after that just compounded the fact that I was a mistake, so it wasn't a very good environment to grow up in. Trying to learn in school was awful because I was a nervous wreck. If I made a mistake, I thought it was just terrible proof that I was a mistake. My dad was physically abusive; he had a really bad temper, and there were unwritten rules that as a child I wasn't aware of and so, if I broke any of those rules I would get beat with a hairbrush, usually to the point of bruising or taking the skin off.

In my childhood, basically I was a loner. Not anything really negative about it, but we didn't show emotion; no hugs and kisses and stuff like that in our house. My dad drank a lot. And he always went to work, but I had to go, basically on the holidays, I had to go to the tavern and drag him home, so he'd be home for Christmas dinner or whatever. My parents never hit us or spanked us or anything like that, but my dad was verbally abusive. There was really no support. I was in the band and they never came to a concert, never came to a football game to watch us march.

In marriage, these mates focused on respect and working together:

We basically had to depend a lot on each other. There were hard times financially, and I took second jobs and sometimes she'd work weekends and nights when I could be home with the kids. We just pulled together as a team.

The secret to a good marriage is honesty. And you have to understand that the other person isn't perfect; there has to be give and take. If the other person doesn't change the way you want, then that means you have to give; you have to be able to say, "I accept this person for who they are" and I think you have to respect their privacy. They have to have an area where they can be by themselves where you're not interrupting them, not stepping in. You have to respect their need to time alone.

You have to allow the other person to be themselves. We really like one another. I also admire him as a person. I respect him; I admire his talents.

There was a time when we just weren't making it. He was so emotionally distant from me. We tried counseling, but it didn't work out. I felt attacked; the counselor betrayed a confidence in group therapy. I left. We had to work it out by ourselves.

<u>Couples low in affection and low in respect.</u> There were some couples who seemed to have struggled always. There was little demonstration of affection or mutual respect. They expressed sadness and anxiety, did not acknowledge each other, and showed little humor. They seemed to avoid any real discussion of their differences. Divorce after 20 years of marriage was rare in our sample, but more likely for couples weak in both affection and respect.

For these couples, there were typically childhood experiences of neglect. The husbands and wives described their own parents as not close emotionally, as rarely showing affection and often arguing. Childhood experiences included poverty and abuse. Often there was a loss of a relationship with a parent, particularly a father who was absent due to death, or just because he was working all the time. So when these couples married, they came into the marriage without good role models for how to create a good marriage. They were also likely to have difficulty forming relationships built on trust. Being fearful, they were likely to describe themselves as having difficulties feeling close to people. They were uncomfortable asking people for help, preferring to do things on their own. Psychologists refer to this as insecure attachment [5]. Yet in our sample, despite all of their difficulties, several of these couples described themselves as happily married.

> *We're complete opposites, but we also managed to agree; we never went to bed mad at each other. We're best friends.* I

don't bother her when she's watching her soap operas. *We talk. If I don't like something, I tell him.*

Well, I'm not gonna say that we've never fought or anything like that, but not to the point where either one of us has left the house or left for days. Never like that. We've never walked out of the house. We've never walked out on each other. We've never been physically abusive to each other. He's never even laid a hand on me. Of course, I have on him (laugh). Just joking. But it's being open and being honest with each other and saying what you feel. Maybe it's luck, and we're just very compatible with each other, and we have been all of these years.

The secret to a good marriage is staying out of her hair (laughs). I go to work so I'm not here. If I didn't work, I'd be a couch potato. (This man was still working over 60 hours a week at the time of our interview; both mates were over 65.)

The secret to a good marriage is not having secrets, doing things together, honesty, and luck.

Dealing with many challenges, these couples chose to hang in, to survive, in spite of difficult childhoods and difficult marriages.

Well, I didn't really have a family structure when I was growing up. I came from a quite well-to-do background, but my mother and father were not happy with one another at all. He wasn't home very often. He'd come for meals, leave early in the morning, come home around four o'clock when my mother would have a meal on the table. Then he would either sleep or change his clothes and leave. I don't know when he would come home. This made my mother very angry and she would sulk. She wanted a divorce very badly, but in those days you didn't divorce. She'd say, "Well, where am I going to go; it's not good for the children." So they stayed together, and he went his own way and she stayed at home and was a very unhappy woman who took everything out on her kids. We were always told we could never do anything right; we were dumb; we couldn't read; we couldn't do this; we couldn't do that. She was very unhappy and took it out on us. I've had repercussions of it all of my life. So money isn't everything. I don't have any contact with any of my siblings. It's just me. So that's why I am the way I am, I believe, and I think that a lot of it goes back to your background. Its things that are instilled in you as a small child. They're ingrained and they gnaw at you through your whole life.

We've had a lot of heartaches in our marriage. It's like getting blood out of a turnip to get him to talk. But he has been a good provider. It was very hard on her when I went to Vietnam and even after I got out. I was gone a lot with my work. It was hard times when I wasn't able to be home very much. *We don't have support systems. I'm not a person that gets close to anybody really. I try to do things on my own. Also, my husband has an alcohol problem and I haven't been able to deal too well with that* *through the years. But he's much better now. I've thought about divorce, but there's just something that that says I can't make it on my own.*

I had a rough childhood. It made me tough. But I have struggled with depression. I'm very religious; we both are. It seems to me that we're all insecure and that a person has to have some kind of a belief system beyond the person.

When asked the secret of a good marriage, these couple emphasized commitment, sticking it out, being there for each other through problems and trouble.

It's like a job. There are days when you might want to quit and run away, but you just stick it out. *That's true.*

Chapter 4

Challenges and Supports

As these couples set out to create families, there were some things that they wanted to do just as their parents had done, and some things they wanted to do differently. They wanted to instill morals in their children as their parents had done for them. Likewise they wanted to carry forward family patterns of trust and caring. They wanted to instill in their children a strong work ethic and the habit of honesty. When asked how they tried to be similar to their parents, they focused on things such as:

- *Respect for the laws of the land*

- *Respect for other people*

- *Provide a strong moral framework for the family*

- *Instill values and honesty*

- *Instill a work/study ethic in the kids*

- *Teach children responsibility*

- *Give children trust*

- *Loving and caring*

When asked how they wanted to be different, they focused on having more emotional closeness with their mate. They wanted more demonstration of affection and better communication in their marriage. And they wanted more education for their children. They also wanted to be more relaxed with children, less strict. They wanted to give them time and listen to them, show them more warmth and caring, and also allow more individuality. Answers to "How did you try to be different from your parents?" included the following:

- *Kiss and hug and touch a lot*

- *Raise good and happy children*

- *Give our children freedom to choose their way in life*

- *Show love and understanding*

- *Not fight or disagree in front of children*

- *More family activities*

- *Communication between parents and children*

Challenges

These couples faced many challenges over the course of their marriage as they tried to create the marriages and families that they desired. The challenges they mentioned mostly had to do with finances and jobs; 70% of the couples mentioned some such challenge. Other oft-mentioned challenges involved illness (39%), caring for children (41%) and concerns involving their own parents (32%). In the quotes, wives' answers are italicized; husbands' are not.

> ***We've had a lot of heartaches in our marriage. We fell in love on a blind date, and basically, we were physically attracted to one another. We didn't know each other even though we were***

engaged for a year...He didn't talk; then came military service; then the job that kept him away from home. So there was lots of stress on me.

The early years were difficult. We were awfully young when we got married; he was still in school, often had to be away, and I had small children. Often, I was home alone with the children and had to get up night after night. Her support allowed me to do what I needed to do so financially we'd be better off. *It was a hard time, but we made it through.*

She didn't finish her degree; then after the kids got a little older, she went back to school and got a teaching certificate. At nights she went back to school. And this was at the time when they were laying teachers off, so she couldn't get a teaching job. So as tough as she is, she went back and got another degree in nursing and became a registered nurse and spent twenty years as a nurse before she retired.

I would say the hardest times were when the children were young. I felt during that time very alone because he worked very long hours and I had three small children which is very stressful. We probably survived that because we came from families that survived. I mean you didn't think in terms of divorce.

For my part, I had a strong feeling, even though we did do a lot of things with our parents, I had a very strong feeling that I wanted to do a lot of things differently from my parents, because there was so much malfunctioning and there was so much guilt and there was so much anger in the family that was never expressed and so on. And I don't know that I did a real good job, but I probably broke a few of the links. And my kids, I'm sure, again I'm hoping, are breaking more of those links so maybe the dysfunction is gradually disappearing.

He was doing the work he wanted to do but starting at the bottom. I remember going to the store. We had one baby and we were expecting another one. And I can remember going to the store in tears and saying, "I can't afford toothpaste and shaving cream, how are we going to afford a new baby?" You have to be young to do that.

I knew I had to work. In the job I had, you had to start at two o'clock in the morning. And the kids were small, and I was working these long six-day weeks, holidays. It put a strain on the family. I was a type A personality. *I think that once he got the financial security he was after, he really did calm down and mellow out.*

When we got married, we had a hard time finding a place to live. There just weren't any good places. *Well, we started out in a hotel, but we couldn't afford that cause you had to get your meals. And then we went into a private home and rented a bedroom. The first year we were married, we lived five places. Next, we shared a little apartment with a couple who were friends of ours and they were renting also. It was like an attic apartment. Then the house next door to his mother's was being rented.* The guy was transferred to New York or something. *For a year we lived there. We* rented a whole house for fifty dollars a month (laugh), which was hard. I was probably making a dollar ten cents an hour at that time. *So starting out, that was very hard, not having a place to live.* I was doing shift work. *Next, we went to a basement apartment at my mom's house. That was supposed to be temporary, but we stayed there seven years until we bought this house. And we had the kids. Our first child was born one year into the marriage.* Then when we bought this house, I had to pay for it. When I think back on it now, it was kind of tough. We never had any money left over for anything. You paid your mortgage, you bought food, and hopefully you had money left for the car so that you could get back and forth to work. It wasn't like it is nowadays, with the wages these people are pulling down. *We really struggled money-wise. Mainly, I think, when I look back, it is that neither one of us were really good at managing money. And at that time, women stayed at home and took care of the children. Now they do it all. They have their jobs and take care of the children and do everything. All my girlfriends, we always stayed home to take care of the children.*

His mom was sick a lot longer than my mom, but that was only the last three years of her life. We lost my brother-in-law, my mother, and his mother within three months of each other. So they were three big losses, and my brother-in-law was younger than my husband and he was gone suddenly in a few days; it was just stunning. My husband helped to take care of his mom; he went to live with his sister and helped take care of his mom, nursed her. My mom had severe health problems on again and off again. But she always came back like the cat with nine lives. Then one time we took her to the hospital thinking she had the flu or something and she died on Mother's Day. She didn't come out and that was a shock.

So we had it both ways. His mom was on an extended illness that we knew was gonna be terminal and my mom, who left after several illnesses. My father-in-law just dropped dead. He had an aneurism and poof he was gone.

When we married, we didn't have nothing. We both worked and we charged all of the furniture and we paid it all off and went forward. *And we never charged after that.* I had three jobs and went to school nights. We just worked together. We lived in an apartment and the landlady said we'd have to move when my wife was pregnant because they didn't allow children there. The thing is that in our relationship we never worried about anybody else and what they had. We've always lived within our means. If there were problems or accidents with the kids, then we accepted them, and we just realized that it's just part of living and growing up. We worked at ways to have fun and to make sure that we were content with what we had. Our neighbors were all in the same boat. We were all our own entertainment. *We always had goals.* We always had plans for better things, and we worked towards them.

Couples often mentioned an upside to a challenge, something they learned or some way that they benefited.

Our son lived at home with us until he was an adult; he never matured at a normal rate. That has been a big part of our life. A good part of our life. It was a challenge, and something that … I don't know how to describe it … it was a very meaningful part of our life. *Our other children were very supportive, and very helpful. I think, also, that it helped them. A lot of our best friends are people we met in support groups for the handicapped that we've been involved in.*

In terms of crisis in our marriage, I would say that one of them was when my mother came to live with us. It was an adjustment for everybody. She was in her late 70s, and she lived here for 10 years before she died. It's always an adjustment when someone comes into

your household, and I don't mean it was all bad. My daughter said "Mom, I don't need two mothers" because my mother did see herself still in the role of mother. But it also opened the way for me to go back to work because eventually I realized that it would be better for everyone if I did. We only had one kitchen and my mother loved to cook. I worked part time for awhile and eventually I went to work full time but since there was someone in the house when the kids came home from school that worked out. I also went back to college. And I couldn't have done that if she hadn't been here. Yet it was difficult to have someone else around. I think that's true in any family where you have someone else come in. I have many friends in my age bracket and this is something. I mean our generation was expected to take care of parents. Today we are determined that we will never live with our children, but we have the options because there is more money now than there was in previous generations. We took in my grandmother when I was a child, and this was an expected thing. Fortunately today it's not that way.

We fought a lot in our younger days. Then I had triple-bypass surgery. I became a different guy. I got myself an altogether different outlook on life. And when you've got a better outlook on life, you make a better life.

When he was in the military, it was just too difficult being married and being separated. We really grew apart, and it was really difficult, especially for my husband. I started drinking. I had friends and family to support me and he was all by himself. And he became a different person that I didn't like. And so when we got back together again there was really nothing left, and so we started rebuilding our relationship from that point. And that was really the worst time in our marriage, AND it was the best time because we were by ourselves. There were no family and friends around us; we could really talk things through, and it became the happiest time. What she's talking about is when I was in the Navy. We weren't together. But then it came a time when she came out there to live with me. We had kind of a duplex. We had nothing, and being so far away, nobody could interfere with our relationship and so that was really the happy part, because we got back together, and we got to understand each other somewhat and we got to go to the beach, and we had plastic curtains in the windows. We had a card table to eat our dinner on. So we had absolutely nothing to speak of, but that was actually a pretty good start cause we were back together again after almost four years apart.

A few people mentioned their own mental health issue or an extramarital affair. It may be that others omitted these topics because it was considered private, not something you discuss with others. This generation seemed to keep more of their life private than is common for many in later generations.

Well, we had one hard time in our marriage, and my wife was very forgiving about it (affair). There was a very definite chance that we'd divorce, but we started counseling and fortunately for both of us the therapist was very competent and helped us through it. And after a couple of years, being led down the mazes of our relationship, we wound up probably with a stronger relationship than we had initially. It was either make or break and there really weren't any other options.

I learned from my Dad about alcohol. I wanted to stay away from alcohol and cigarettes because they were bad for my father and for my parents' relationship. But I learned to drink from him and became a good alcoholic, took a run through the treatment center and ten years of AA, and I've been sober now for twenty years. But I drank for twenty before that. I think it was the employer that finally got me motivated to get help. Cause they said that either it's get help or lose your job.

We had a lot of lows. His mother died, then a few years later, his father and it bothered him quite a bit. He had a nervous breakdown. I was in depression. *About ten years ago, my mother had Alzheimer's and it was extremely stressful. It all came to a head one night. That was probably the worst thing in my life.* We clash. Our personalities clash. We seem to work it out one way or another, even though she doesn't talk. *We ended up having a major battle when I was stressed about my mother, which I think, with a lot of people it could have ended up in divorce, but it didn't. We went to counseling. I wanted him to read my mind and I don't say much. He does more talking. I'm very sensitive and he's not.* Well, when my father died, I had several bouts with depression. But after the first one I kind of knew how to handle it better. My father suffered from depression, but he didn't treat it. My wife was a big help. We love each other, we don't just like each other.

Supports

We asked the couples how they managed, what kind of supports they had. The most common answers to this question were friends (63%), family (54%), each other (42%), and faith or church (39%):

> *We always had a good neighborhood, so we always had close relationships with our neighbors, and our children kind of grew up together.* We've had the stability of living in the same place.

> **I *remember one time when my husband was out of own and I just needed time by myself to soak in the tub for awhile, and my mother sent my brother over to get the kids and bring them to her.* We always lived close to families.**

> *There was a group of us from the church choir, five couples. We would take vacations together, so our kids grew up together. We're having a reunion next*

summer, us, our kids, cats and dogs, everything.

We've got good friends. Very good friends, neighbors. We moved here about thirty years ago...the original people that moved out here with us are still here. *Yea, about five couples left. We still go out for Christmas parties, and get together.* And summer, we always go out for a summer outing.

We lived one year in an apartment. We moved above my in-laws for two or three years and then we moved here. *My folks lived next door. We bought the two houses.* Well, when they found out I was looking at a house, they said you can't move without us. And I said I don't want to live in the same house...so we bought lots together and built two houses. I would say it worked out very well. I mean sure we have our differences and that, but never any real arguments. *And it was often convenient to send the kids over there when we wanted to go out. It was a good support that way. We ate dinner together. They worked all the time. They came home and had dinner with us and then they went to their house. So I mean it was a good relationship all the way through.*

We had a large extended family. In time of stress, we could go to them. I feel that's one of today's major problems. So often there isn't a really large family network that can be there for each other, and I guess maybe other people have their friends as being their support system, but in our case, I'd have to say that it's mostly family.

I did a lot of praying one time. *Saint Jude. I used to pray to him all the time when something seemed hopeless.* We used to go to church, and it was important to me. *I go once in a while.* She's mad at the church because the nuns made her mad and all that crap. *Well, I had a Catholic upbringing.* So did I. But she took things too seriously — all that stuff about limbo when you're in the sixth grade. Yea, the church was a good thing. But some of the people that represent the church were a little bizarre. They told me Jews had horns when I was little. My father had a client who was Jewish, and he used to come over for dinner, and I was actually looking at his head for horns. And I was thinking, "This is crazy; somebody is nuts here; this man has got no horns; I don't think these people know what they're talking about."

We had friends. *All of our neighbors were in the same boat, struggling financially like us. We'd get together and play cards, and we'd all chip in and maybe somebody would buy some beer. It wasn't like anybody was above you, you were all in the same boat. We had small children. We'd go to the beach at nights or have cookouts. I think we had kind of pleasant early years. I remember I was terrified of storms. I had a very loving and considerate neighbor, and during a storm when my husband wasn't home, they would leave their door open and I could go over there (laugh).*

We had friends and family, but our primary support was each other because we didn't necessarily go out of our household to seek support. Everybody else has got their own problems, and they're not listening to yours.

PART II: SUCCESSFUL LIFELONG MARRIAGE

Researchers who have studied successful marriages find several common themes: commitment, trust, communication and conflict management skills, similar values, religion, doing things together, love, understanding, and willingness to forgive [6, 7, 9, 11, 12]. Also important are childhood family experiences, communication skills, how mates' personalities, values, faith traditions and goals for marriage fit with each other [8]. In this part of the book, we will see what these couples, married over 40 years, have to say about what is most important in marriage. After asking them about their own marriage we asked what they thought was important for a successful marriage.

Chapter 5

Integrity, Trust, Commitment

Over half of the couples we interviewed stressed the importance of integrity, the ability to trust each other, and the need for commitment to the marriage. They often expressed the opinion that people today are too quick to call it quits. In the quotes, wives' answers are italicized; husbands' are not.

> Young people getting married have got the attitude that if *we don't agree then we just get divorced, and I don't think you can start a relationship with that idea. You've got to have patience.* You've got to understand that there are gonna be disagreements and you've gotta iron 'em out. You can't fight 'em with your hat on, let's put it that way.

> *I talked to a girl once, and like almost everybody in her family was divorced. She was married, but her attitude was, like, if this doesn't work, I'm just gonna get divorced. That was her attitude*

going in. It seems so foreign to me. I didn't know anybody who was divorced.

The most important thing is mutual respect. I never underestimate his abilities and I don't think he never underestimates mine.

Well I think mutual attraction is most important. And there has to be honesty and trust and cooperation. *And the woman has to be able to bend. There's a two-way street. Both have to bend. People today are not willing to go through the bad times to get to the good times. I don't call it independence and I don't call it education. If you're smarter, you should know you're gonna have good times and bad times. There's no utopia.*

The secret to a good marriage is working at it. You can't take each other for granted; give and take. And when they talk about who is your best friend, obviously your mate should be your best friend. You should be able to talk to one another. When our children got married, I said I'll give you one piece of advice, work at your marriage every day cause when you stop, that's it. It's a lot of doing what you say you're gonna do and really commit to something. By God if I say I'm gonna do it, then it gets done.

You have to be trustworthy and it really doesn't take a lot more than that. *You have to believe that there is a person in the marriage that is always going to be honest with you and faithful to you, and you can't expect perfection. And you need a sense of humor. We still have fun together and I think that's important, but I think it's the trust in each other that really matters. And knowing that person's always behind you. If you goof up or something, that it's not gonna change the way you feel about each other.*

I think one thing that may be a little different nowadays is that when we went into marriage, we went into it with the expectation that this is for life. And we didn't really see it as a trial to see if it would work. And I think from that standpoint, I think that it was a trust for each of us that this was it. And I think it was up to us to make it as good or as bad as it was going to be. But it was not that we were going to look to something else. This was going to be it. Stick together for the good things and the bad things, the good times and the bad times.

When I went into the marriage, I assumed it was gonna be forever and then when all the troubles came along, to me they seemed like they were small compared to this overarching "this isn't gonna change." So we had to work it out kind of thing. I think also that as far as stability of the family, it's come to me, now that I'm older, we both came from families where we had both parents alive, well, and together; they stuck it out.

The secret of a good marriage is not keeping anything from each other. Giving your true feelings and discussing things whether you feel bad or good about it, you know, doing things together, not being secretive, not holding anything back, having your mate as your best friend, you know, and just not keeping anything from each other, any secrets or hiding anything, financial or whatever it might be, or if you buy something or anything, whatever it might be, even the smallest thing. That's what it is for me.

The secret to a good marriage is that you have to be trustworthy. *You have to believe that the other person in the marriage is always going to be honest. But you can't expect perfection. I think it's the trust in each other that really matters.*

Chapter 6

Affection, Caring, Support and Respect

The couples stressed both affection and respect. A few mentioned sex, but this is a more private generation. In the quotes, wives' answers are italicized; husbands' are not.

I think that being friends is most important. And the attitude that you're in it for life and the little tings aren't gonna split you apart. You're gonna stick it through those difficult times and be there for support. Loyalty. I think that's an important thing, that you're loyal to each other. I never had a doubt in my mind that if something was important to me, and that I wanted to do it, that she wouldn't support me, never.

One thing that comes to mind is allowing each other to have their own interests. And their own lives besides the marriage. So you each have to have things that you can do independently, as well as things you can do together.

I think being a support for the other person when the need is there is very important. I think we found invariably when one person was down, the other person just picks them right up. That was that kind of thing that happened with us almost automatically, and that was pretty important. One person would really be angry or down about something and the other person would be able to help 'em to see why it wasn't so good or be cheerful or something that would counterbalance it. *And the support that you had is because we both knew that no matter what, the other would support us and would not badmouth us to the kids or the grandparents or friends or whatever. That we could always count on that loyalty even if you were temporarily lying (laugh). That counts as support.* In terms of raising the kids we always supported one another so when the kids would try to play one off the other, as they would do from time to time, we would always say, "What did Dad or Mom say? Well that's the way it'll be then."

Like I said, we didn't really have a clue when we married, but I do think that both of us make an effort to keep our love alive. I'm not necessarily talking about sexual things, but a day doesn't go by that we don't hug each other.

Two people have to like each other. We like each other basically. The bottom line is that we like each other. We don't always get along, but we like each other. I don't want to get rid of her or anything like that, and she doesn't want to get rid of me.

Sex is important in a good marriage. It's the best part of our marriage. It's the only thing that's lasted for forty years. *Yes, sex is very important. We've always had good chemistry. We've always had good chemistry for sex. Not always for other things, but for that.*

You have to be honest and you have to understand that the other person is not perfect and that there has to be give and take. I think you have to understand that you have to be able to say, "I accept this person for who they are," and I think you have to respect their time alone and their privacy. *We really like one another. Don't marry anyone that you don't basically like and respect as a person.*

Understanding is important, understanding and patience. Knowing that we all have faults and that no one is perfect. And forgiveness. Forgiveness is very important.

You've got to be there for each other. Be there if you really need them. We realize that each person needs some time by themselves. You can't just live with each other and stay on top of each other all the time.

Chapter 7

Similarity, Complementarity and Couple Time

Is it better to marry someone similar to yourself – same background, ethnicity, religion, interests? Or do opposites attract? These couples say that both are important. In the quotes, wives' answers are italicized; husbands' are not.

He's better at getting things out in the open. I'm more optimistic, he's more pessimistic. I think the balance between us being a little different in those areas kind of helps our marriage. I think when I get upset about something, he doesn't and vice versa…then we can meet in the middle of the table.

We have lots of things in common like our faith. And goals. We have similar interests, things we like to do together. But we have dissimilar interests, too, which makes it a little more exciting.

You know our relationship has changed dramatically over time. In our younger years he was the ruler of the household, and in our older years I am the ruler of the household. He's been retired for several years now and he does exactly what he wants, when he wants, and I run everything else. So I say this or that and he goes along with it, whereas in the past he was the ruler of the household and I went along with him. The power has shifted. I'm more tolerant now. Now if I was the same as her, we wouldn't be here today. *Well I'm in total agreement. Before I was the one who was more tolerant, and he was the one who made demands. Now he is the one who works hard, and I am the one who makes demands. So there's always that balance in the relationship, and so we're always in agreement that there has to be a balance. We can't both be at the same place. Earlier, he was the one responsible for maintaining the financial needs of our family and I was responsible for raising and disciplining the children. Now we don't have financial needs. I continue to work* because I enjoy it and he pursues his pleasures. That's our lifestyle now.

Well, he is more childlike. He can have fun in all kinds of situations, and he doesn't worry so much as I do. So it was calming, and playful. But I'm more serious; I like to get things done. So we complement each other. He eases me up and I might tighten him up a little bit.

We rarely are upset at the same time. We're upset about different things at different times, and that works out beautifully. There was one time when I was in the final stages of a pregnancy in the summer time, and he was sick, and it was a very rough time … and that really brought to mind how much we usually support each other.

We come from very different backgrounds. In spite of everything, we have a common thing, we both love our kids dearly. We may disagree on a lot of things. But I think on our philosophy of life and morals and that type of thing, I

think we're totally in sync. We think alike in that way although we very much differ sometimes when it comes to politics. Basically, we have the same philosophy of life.

We're complete opposites really. I mean he's Protestant, I'm Catholic. He's Republican; I'm Democrat. I've got more of a hot temper than he has. I'm more frugal than he is. I'm the spend thrift (laugh). *But we always agreed; we never really went to bed mad at each other.* Right, and our interests are the same. We discuss things if we have a disagreement; I think we talk things out pretty well. We're best friends. *Right.*

Not being so vocal, I guess. Going along with the vocal one. Well, I think a real successful marriage is one in which both of you aren't aggressive. One of you has got to be the give-in guy. Cause if you've got two aggressive people... **Well, no competition if that's what you mean; one has to be more easy going. My father was from the old country and**

he was the boss. Of course, my mom was from the old country, too, and she went along with it.

We agree about almost everything. We both have pretty much the same ethnic background; maybe that's helpful. And the same religious background, although it's not overpowering in our lives. And neither one of us has hot tempers. It's also important to spend time together.

It's important to do things with your kids, go to their concerts and stuff. But it's also important to do couple things. Kids need to have a bedtime. Then there's time for the parents to spend together. It's important to have individual interests, too. I'd go fishing with the guys; she would do things with her sisters, "sister weekends" at least once a year.

A lot of the time, when both parents are working, it's hard to have a regular bedtime for the children because you want the time with them. But you have to have your own time in the evening with your husband. You can't just always let the children take priority.

Mostly we did things with the kids, but we also had groups, like we belonged to a square-dancing group and a bridge group. We belonged to different groups that met as couples.

I think that with our age group, a lot of times the guys would say that raising children is a woman's job, but my husband always took part. If I put 'em to bed, he would do the dishes; if I did the dishes, he'd get them ready for bed so we would have some time together.

Chapter 8

Communication, Compromise and Humor

Seventy percent of couples mentioned something about communication, problem solving, compromise. Interestingly enough, many talked about letting things go. You can't solve every problem and you don't need to. In the quotes, wives' answers are italicized; husbands' are not.

We scream at each other sometimes. Don't go to bed without resolving it. We usually scream at each other and get it over with. We don't feel the same way about things. But eventually I think we find out that it doesn't make any difference. It's not important.

Well I think identifying your problem is one thing, but solving it is another. I don't think you can solve anything by just turning it inward and not laying it out on the table. I think you've just gotta be forward and say "This is how I feel because if we do this, I think this is

gonna happen. What do you think?" I think you've just got to be open to the other person's side. I tell young kids today, I tell 'em divorce is too easy and you don't just start the race and say "Oh, I don't want to do this." *Well you should never expect to have your own way all the time in life so why would you expect it in marriage. I mean it's unreasonable to expect that you're always gonna have you own way. You don't do it at work, you don't do it with the government, you don't do it with the police, why would you expect to do it with your spouse? By the other token, you can expect to be treated like an intelligent human being. If you're being misused or you don't feel that you are being accepted as an intelligent human being with your own rights, then you do have a problem.*

I think the secret of marriage is communication and not holding back. I mean we don't hold back and there's no real secrets. You just let it all out. We really don't argue. We yell at each other sometimes, but it's not anything that lasts. Nothing is that important. It's over with. We might say something but it's over with right then. It doesn't harbor for several days. I think a lot of it is knowing when to keep quiet and bringing it up sometimes later. *Well, maybe you do that; I let it out right away (laughs).* And you've just got to let some things go because you aren't going to be able to change them. So why bother arguing about it.

We didn't have time to fight. We didn't see each other that much. Well, we didn't want to fight. My parents fought when I was a child and I remember that, and it didn't accomplish nothing. *He blows up and then I'll look at him and then he'll calm down. As fast as he blows up, he calms down.* Once you get it off your chest; it's all gone.

Communication. You have to tell him what you want, and he has to tell you what he wants. It may not always work out, but at least you've got to know. I think that's the only way you can really get along. When everything is calmed down, just to say and talk about it.

You need to solve your internal problems together, not with family or friends. Neither of us went to seek counsel from parents. We tried to settle things ourselves and discuss them and work it out for ourselves. Cause what was good for our parents isn't necessarily good for our marriage and our family. In those days, you have to remember, you didn't have Border's self-help books telling you how to be a wife, how to be a mother.

Communicating. Another thing is that with our children we tried to stick together. Personally and privately we may have disagreed with each other, but we never argued in front of them. *We tried to teach them respect for themselves and for other people.*

I think if you'll give from one side and he'll give from the other side then it

works out. But you can't always be right. Even if you think you're right, you might just bite your tongue a little bit once in a while. It doesn't hurt, you know.

Take buying things. We always come home and say, 'let's sleep on it.' *We don't have to agree. Sometimes it's one person's idea. You know, I might not particularly like it, but I'll go along with it because it's kind of a compromise. I think compromise is very important in a relationship. You can't always get your own way.*

I came from a family where the father was the last word. So all the power was vested in the male. And as I got older, I came to realize that that led to a lot of anger on my part that I wasn't aware of. I think I was angry right out of the box because of that. At the same time, early in the marriage she gave in more in terms of compromising. I was more dogmatic in my feelings and harder to change because, I think, underneath she had a far greater feeling of basic

security than I did, and I came out feeling not secure and covered it up by trying to be right about everything. But you've got to compromise, not be so rigid, give and take. You have to care about each other, love each other. It has to be important enough to make the sacrifices, or else it just doesn't go.

Humor was mentioned as important to a successful marriage by about a fourth of the couples.

You've gotta be able to find humor in life and situations in life or you're gonna just wind up all in knots.

We get along. We always have and we both have a sense of humor and we do lots of teasing and kidding and things like that. We do that with our family, our children, our grandchildren. I think that helps too. And the people that we know are that way. Our friends that we keep company with, they all have a fairly good sense of humor and now we don't get into nasty teasing because

sometimes it can get over the [limit]. But that's just the way we are.

The secret to a good marriage is respecting each other; being there when you need 'em. *Yea, and not crowing. Don't be like cling on type of thing; or being the boss –* you do this; you do that. Love and affection are important, too… and humor. We kid around a lot. *And since the kids have left, we work together a lot. I load the dishwasher, he unloads it (laugh). I make dinner; he clears off the table.*

Chapter 9

Friends, Family, Faith, and Finances

Faith, friends and family were also considered to be important. Couples mentioned these issues when they talked about the support they had to help them through life. And several mentioned the importance of money. In the quotes, wives' answers are italicized; husbands' are not.

We're lucky to have some really good friends that like the same things we do and that's a part of our marriage that's very nice. And our relatives. We see them a lot, our nephews. And we came up in the same church. It helps when a lot of things are similar, families that have the same backgrounds.

I still keep up with the girls I went to grade school with.

I think the important thing is faith and your church. And you have to respect the other person. Now you know that life is not a rose garden and you're gonna have to have problems. We've always gone to church on Sundays together, and it was keeping us together. We always took the kids to church, even Mary, our party girl for a while. She knew that no matter how late she stayed out, she had to get up and go to church with Mom and Dad the next day. That was it; this family went to church.

Church is important. And friends. We started going on vacation with this other couple that we travel with every summer. *We've been going with them for forty years.* We each had a cabin years ago, you know, one for each family. And when the kids were all gone on both sides, we stayed together in one cabin.

After we each finished school and had careers, finances were not a problem. When I look back to my family as a child, one big difference is finances. That has allowed us to do many things that my parents could not do. I think the greatest compliment I could give my parents is that we were poor, and I never knew it.

Things got easier as we got more money.

Money is important too and the making of it, of course. But being able to agree on what to do with it -- the values and stuff -- because we didn't have tons of money when the kids were young. And we gave up some things. I didn't have the best wardrobe in the world or something, maybe to make sure that the kids could get involved in things, and that took a lot of money. And I think the fact that we never went out and bought something big without talking. Like he would never go out and buy a new set of golf clubs without our talking. We'd agree that we can't afford this, and we'll do that instead. I think it's important to agree on how you're spending your money.

One half of marriages don't work out because of money. Some people have unreal expectations, and for others it just doesn't work out. They don't work

out their finances and that's bad. That puts a lot of pressure and a lot of stress on the marriage. It takes a hell of a marriage to survive without a good financial basis. People have to feel secure about something in this world, and women, especially have to feel secure about it. I believe that. *That's true. I agree that women want to be secure. And I think they want to be independent, too. I believe in women working. I didn't work full time very long, but I did a lot of part time work.*

I don't think money is everything, but it certainly is important. Anybody who says money isn't anything or doesn't count, then they're not thinking very clearly because if you think of the stress, finances or lack of decent finances put you under, that has to affect your relationship with each other, too. I think if you have enough money to get along and you're not behind on your bills, it helps a lot.

The secret of a good marriage is compatibility, doing things together.

Being good friends. We both think a lot about problems nowadays with more breakups in family -- maybe due to two different jobs. One person staying home (either wife or husband) can help a lot. *Well, I think that women have become too independent. And this goes way back to my parents because my mother always said that a mother's place is home with the children. And sure, we could always use more money, but did we really need it? Everybody says that they need two jobs, but everything's relative. ... Even when you don't have money you can get together and play bridge or whatever you want to do. We took the kids with us and our friends brought their kids to our house. We brought the kids to each other's houses because we couldn't afford babysitters (laughs). It was fifty cents an hour.*

Chapter 10

A Few Final Thoughts

Sometimes it's hard to get perspective on our own life or on our own generation. Looking back in time can give us perspective. These couples grew up during a depression and were raised by parents who had little education. Many of their parents were immigrants who had to learn a new language when they came to the United States. In this parental generation, 30% did not attend high school; only about 50% graduated high school. We can see the very large increase in education from one generation to the next. Of the people in our study, 95% graduated high school; 25% graduated college. If we look at the next generation, all of their children graduated high school; and 70% graduated from college.

Those who grew up during the depression have a lot to teach us; a lot of things they learned are applicable to marriages today. Commitment, honesty, affection, respect, good communication. Perhaps these are the basics. Staying connected, respecting each other, supporting and receiving support from our families, friends and faith communities, these things can help us all survive and thrive. In the quotes, wives' answers are italicized; husbands' are not.

> We've been very, very fortunate. When something is going wrong, seems like something comes along and goes right and balances out. And I don't think either of us spends out lives feeling sorry for ourselves, which kind of helps.

> *You have to agree on what your goals are. You have to agree on your children and the way that you're raising them. And in my case, you overlook the little things. It's not worth getting hung up on little things. Don't fall apart on little things, wait for the big ones to come. And then, I think you can handle it much better. I'm very positive. I'm a positive person. With me, it's always the glass half full. I do not judge anybody without knowing them. I always expect the best.*

From a couple who suffered financial setbacks and job losses, multiple illnesses (heart attack, cancer), difficulties with children during adolescence, loss of siblings through death and difficult relationships with one parent:

I don't think we're anything other than average people as far as good times, bad times. It's how you deal with things that counts.

A disabled child was born to this couple when their other children were in their teens. The husband had an operation for cancer:

Sometimes when I went to the doctors, they were surprised that I could hold the attitude I had. One doctor said that some people that had the same problem that I had took it too much to heart and were angry or upset about it, and let it ruin their lives. I don't know that we really let anything ruin our lives for any length of time – no matter what. Even with raising a disabled child -- that was the major challenge. But we seem to be able to work around things a lot. Work together.

Other Comments:

Patience is the secret to a good marriage. Listen before you speak. I think that's the most important. **I think you've got to both agree that whatever your destiny is going to be, you have to work together to get it. And you cannot be selfish. You have to eliminate selfishness. You just can't do it. And you have to work together to do everything, every project, every goal has to be a mutual agreement, or it just won't work. We accepted our limitations.** *It wasn't that important to have a big house, to have a new car. When we got something, we enjoyed it, but it really wasn't that important.* **It's easy for the kids today to walk away**

from marriage. We were brought up with the idea that sure you have problems, but you work 'em out, and you just don't say "hey, I'm going on." We're not saying that you don't have arguments; you have turmoil now and then, which is good and healthy, I think, and you've gotta do that. But the answer isn't walking away.

My problem in life has always been that I like to get to the bottom line. I like to cut through all the red tape and all the other garbage and get to the bottom line. I mean, is it Yes or No. But life is not yes or no, it's not black and white. I mean it's made up of a lot of things and I realize that now. The trouble is that if I'd known at twenty-one what I know at seventy (laughs), I'd have been a hell of a lot better off. ... The problem is that you have to learn where to give; you have to give up something. And I don't mean charity. Sometimes your views, sometimes your feelings, sometimes what you're thinking about, sometimes your own priorities. It's flexibility. That's basically my philosophy of life – that you've got to bend a little bit. You can't just stand there straight and tell everybody to do it your way. That doesn't work.

Of course as your children get older, I shouldn't use the word confining, but I was more concerned when they got older that they were supervised. When your kids are teenagers, you can't just go away for the weekend. From that time, we turned our lives over to the kids so to speak, and they had parties and their friends were always welcome here. We were always home for the parties. We were mom and dad to a lot of kids.

You talk. If something is really bothering you, you let the other person know. If you like something they do, you should let them know. If you're unhappy, I think you really have to confront the person with it and say this is not working. And the second part of that is you have to try to compromise. You can't just make ultimatums and say, "we'll do it my way or no way." You have to somehow work it out. It's the ability of both parties to move, to change. That was important because we're both very, very bullheaded in a lot of ways. What's hardest for you to change, that's what you have to change. Cause the little things change themselves. The marriage evolves. You've gotta grow up together. *Which we pretty well did. We were pretty much kids when we got married.*

We have a mystery period of about ten years where we can't really tell you what happened or why, or how it stopped. But from about the time that we were married thirty years to the time when we were married forty years, we just.... we just weren't making it. We tried counseling, and that was not at all helpful, more a hindrance. So we just had to do it on our own. You have to admit to yourself that you have some bad points about yourself. Some people can't admit that they're wrong. It's hard to admit that you're not perfect. "I'm good, you're not." When you can admit

that you're wrong and say, "I know what I need to do, and as much as I hate to do it, I'm gonna do it," then you can make some progress. And it's not really that I'm gonna do this to save our marriage, you're doing it to save yourself. You have to decide what you really want. But if you don't want to blame yourself and don't want to hold yourself for the way you are, then you're in trouble.

REFERENCES

www.familylegacies.net

[1] Bell, L. G. and Harsin, A. (2018). A prospective longitudinal study of marriage from midlife to later life, Couple and Family Psychology: Research and Practice, 7, 12-21.

[2] Bell, L. G., Meyer, J., Rehal, D., Swope, C, Martin, D. and Lakhani, A. (2007) Connection and Individuation as separate and independent processes: A qualitative analysis, Journal of Family Psychotherapy, *18*, 43-59.

[3] Bell, L. D. & D. C. Bell (2012). Positive relationships that support elder health and wellbeing are grounded in midlife/adolescent family. Family and Community Health, *35*, 276-286.

[4] Bell, L. G. and Bell, D. C. (2005) Family dynamics in adolescence affect midlife well-being, Journal of Family Psychology, *19*, 198-207

[5] Bowlby, J. (1988). *A Secure Base: Parent-Child Attachment and Healthy Human Development*. London: Routledge.

[6] Fenell, D. L. (1933). Characteristics of long-term first marriages. Journal of Mental Health Counseling, *15*, 446-460.

[7] Gottman, J. M & Silver, N. (1999). *The Seven Principles for Making Marriage Work*. New York: Three Rivers Press.

[8] Larson, J. F. (2000). *Should We Stay Together?* New York: Josey-Bass.

[9] Laure, R. H., Lauer, J. C. & Kerr, S. T. (1990). The long-term marriage: Perceptions of stability and satisfaction. International Journal of Aging and Human Development, *31*, 189-195.

[10] Lindenmeyer, K. (2005). *The Greatest Generation Grows Up*, Chicago: Ivan R. Dee.

[11] Waite, L. & Gallagher, M. (2000). *The Case for Marriage: Why Married People are Happier, Healthier, and Better Off Financially*. New York: Doubleday.